How to Pick Pockets for Fun and Profit

A Magician's Guide to Pickpocket Magic

Eddie Joseph

PICCADILLY BOOKS
COLORADO SPRINGS, COLORADO

Cover design and illustrations by Michael Donahue
Text edited and enlarged by Bruce Fife

Piccadilly Books
P.O. Box 25203
Colorado Springs, CO 80936
U.S.A.

Library of Congress Cataloging-in-Publication Data

Joseph, Eddie.
    How to pick pockets for fun and profit: a magician's guide
to pickpocket magic/ Eddie Joseph.
        p.   cm.
    ISBN 0-941599-18-3 (U.S.) -- ISBN 1-85729-015-1 (U.K.)
    1. Tricks. 2. Pickpockets. I. Title.
GV1556.J67 1992
793.8--dc20   91-47019

Simultaneously published in the U.S.A. and the U.K.

TABLE OF CONTENTS

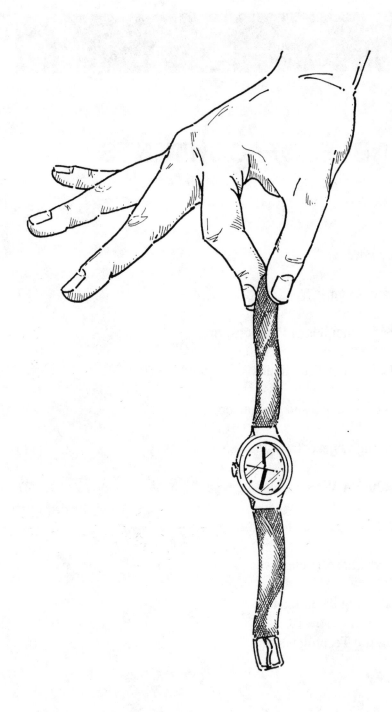

FOREWORD

Eddie Joseph can be classified as one of the most popular magicians of the twentieth century. He has developed his pickpocketing skills to an extraordinary level, spending many years perfecting his craft and entertaining audiences with it. A pickpocket on the street will only steal when no one is looking. Joseph, on the other hand, has done it without detection in front of thousands of people.

Pickpocketing techniques are actually very simple and do not require great sleight-of-hand skill. After reading this book and gaining an understanding of the basic principles of pickpocketing, you will be able to successfully pick pockets.

In this book you will learn techniques for stealing wallets, jewelery, and clothing from unsuspecting people and have fun doing it. I would like to emphasize that the methods discussed in this book are for *entertainment purposes only.* This book was written for those who want to learn a skill to entertain with and should be used only for that purpose.

Using the techinques described in this book will add novelty and variety to an otherwise ordinary magic show. The show will become more memorable, and you will become more popular. As you will discover, a great deal of comedy and enjoyment can be derived from using pickpocket magic. Consequently, pickpocket effects can mean more *fun* for the audience and more *profit* for you. For this reason, the book is titled *How to Pick Pockets for Fun and Profit*.

—Bruce Fife, Editor

INTRODUCTION

Many years ago while visiting in India, I had an interesting experience. I was attending the Indian National Exposition in Calcutta. Being a professional magician, I was attracted to an entertainment section of the fair called "The Magic Theater."

Men, women, and children were streaming toward the theater. Above the noise of the crowd a voice was calling from the direction of the theater, "Come and see what Mabel is doing." Lifting my eyes to locate its source, I gazed upon the figure of a magician who by then had already created quite a stir in this hard-to-please city of magicians and mystics. Towering well above the crowd on a raised platform, the magician continued to draw the crowd—magnetically—to fill his theater. This magician was the famous Percy Abbott.

My attention was attracted by a stalwart form elbowing his way through the mass of humanity, shouting, "He is darn clever, this fellow. I must see him again." He had hardly reached the door of the theater when he returned again, shouting, "I've been pinched! Someone has lifted my purse." "Who could it be?" inquired someone. "How should I know?" replied the unfortunate gentleman, "all I know is that he was swifter than any magician."

This man's misfortune, contrary to expectation, did not draw any sympathy, but produced only hilarity. The people were tickled to death to see this bold gentlemen deprived of his wallet. They found fun in his calamity.

But for me, it was the beginning of a strange idea. Here was a man who lost his money, yet he could not help admiring the perpetrator of this crime. "He is swifter than any Magician," but magicians are supposed to have earned the reputation of having the swiftest hands of any mortal beings.

Magicians are like bloodhounds; when they start on a trail to develop a new trick or gimmick they don't stop untill they reach their goal. I immediately saw the possibility of employing the methods of the pickpocket for entertainment purposes. Using my professional knowledge of misdirection and sleight-of-hand, I developed the methods described in this book. I have incorporated pickpocket magic into my shows with great success and to the bewilderment of many good-natured subjects and audiences. To anyone who would add this branch of entertainment—for entertainment it certainly is—to his regular program, instantaneous success will reward his efforts. The practice of picking pockets for entertainment purposes is by no means difficult. You have to understand the underlying principles of it first. The rest comes easy. I will try and be as clear as possible in my instruction, and if you follow it closely, you will not go wrong.

1

BASIC PRINCIPLES
OF PICKPOCKETING

People believe that the pickpocket can go about his business nonchalantly under all conditions. This is a fallacy. He is bound by limitations the same as the magician is.

Nobody is ever pickpocketed out in the wide open spaces. It simply cannot be done. When you hear of someone being victimized, it was in a crowd—while boarding a bus or plane, moving along in a hurry and accidentally colliding against someone—or under some other similar circumstances.

It is a psychological fact that the human mind can only be conscious of one thing at a time. We may imagine we can think of several things concurrently but it is not so. The man elbowing his way through a crowd has only one immediate aim in his mind, that of reaching his destination. The man boarding a bus is occupied with the fear of missing it. The man in a hurry has his mind filled with the thought of being on time, and the person who has just experienced a collision is too indignant to think of anything else. Whatever the circumstances, the mental state in each case is the same. The mind is preoccupied according to circumstances. The victim's thought, at the crucial moment, is focused in another direction. Psychological law therefore, facilitates the pickpocket's operations. In other words, the victim's mental state becomes a powerful accessory to his own victimization. Without this factor, the pickpocket would never survive.

How many times have you experienced this mental state? Have you never felt oblivious to your surroundings at some time or another when occupied with some distant thought? When our minds are preoccupied, we become less aware of the things around us and can even become immune to minor pain. For instance, have you ever accidentally cut yourself without realizing it? Only after noticing the cut later, when your mind is clear, do you feel the pain. We have all experienced this condition of the mind many times.

As the soil has to be tilled before the seed can be sown, the natural tendency of our mind does the tilling for the pickpocket. He is presented a rich and ready soil to do the sowing.

This explains that in the first and the most important part of picking a pocket the operator plays no part. He merely takes advantage of the mental condition of the victim at the psychological moment. We shall now examine the role the pickpocket actually plays to complete the operation.

The pickpocket's work, in certain respects, bears comparison to that of the magician. By this I mean he appears to be doing something, and under cover of this open action, he fulfills his ulterior desire. In exemplification of this, we shall look into one of his most common practices. The pickpocket begins his lifting operation by "accidentally" colliding against his victim. The moment of the impact affords an ideal cover. Simultaneously with the impact his task is accomplished. The movement of his hand to the pocket is not felt; it is absorbed by the force of the impact.

For a personal experience of this principle, I suggest you place something in your outer coat pocket. Arrange for a friend to walk up and collide against you. He need not be violent as that is not necessary. At the moment of impact he should reach into your pocket and draw out the article. When he does this, you will not feel the movement of his hand. Your mental state, of course, will not play any part in this tryout because you already had previous knowledge of his intention. The bodily impact will dull the sensation caused by the movement of his hand to your pocket. Why? The reason is set out in the next paragraph.

It is a little known fact that the sensation resulting from a greater force, supersedes that of a lesser force. To understand this point, hold a match stick in your left hand and clench your right hand into a fist. First push the point of the match into the flesh of your uncovered thigh. You will be well aware of that thrust. Now let both hands work in unison. The right fist hits the thigh sharply and the left repeats the jab with the match. You will only feel the blow and not the jab. Why? Because the blow is sharper than the thrust. Now if you were to allow someone to hit you on the same spot with a sledge hammer while you use your fist, then the impact of the hammer would supersede that of the blow. It is the case of a weaker force succumbing to the stronger. In plainer language, the greater force numbs the weaker sensation to the extent that you don't feel it at all. However queer this analogy may seem to you, it is here for a definite purpose. This purpose will be evident when we study the practical side of pickpocketing.

Having come this far, it becomes clear that the pickpocket can only operate under the right condition. This condition he has to seek. As the magician does not seek but creates his own conditions, he is in a superior position over the street pickpocket and can create some marvelous effects for entertainment. The correct mental state or a condition of the mind, as we understand, is the reaction to our effort at *misdirection*. As this principle, by long usage, becomes second nature to the magician, is it any wonder at all why we are able to hold any member of the audience on whom we are operating in a vice-like grip? Then again, who understands the full significance of the "coverage principle" better than we do?

The two basic principles you need to know are (1) the subject's mind must be preoccupied and unsuspecting, (2) when removing something from a pocket, mask the movement with a stronger, seemingly innocent, force. Both of these conditions are created by the magician.

We have seen that the pickpocket has to work under cover of some open action. He cannot just walk up to a person, help himself to what he wants, and then retire. We employ the same ruse.

We entertain the audience. Our tricks form the instrument of entertainment, and consequently we make the instrument serve as our shield. Could anything be more natural than this? It would be absurd for me to suggest specific tricks to precede each "lifting" operation. Each of us thinks and works differently. For this reason, I will leave it up to you to choose your own tricks and patter which will lead up to picking your volunteer's pocket.

I can serve you best by describing the moves I employ and which, in my constant practice, I have found to be suitable for the purpose which they are designed. All I am concerned with is teaching the simplicity of pocket lifting when employed for entertainment purposes.

To add to the hilarity, some parts of the operation can be conducted in a manner to make the audience aware of your intentions. They are allowed to see you, for instance, stealing the volunteer's handkerchief. As the volunteer, at no stage, gets the slightest inkling of the procedure, the laughter increases with each successive operation. I will show you how to deal with the stolen articles later. For the present, it will suffice to explain how to relieve the volunteer of his belongings without him or the audience knowing that you have taken possession of them.

2

MISDIRECTION TECHNIQUES

Whether you are picking pockets or doing any other type of magic, you must use misdirection to be successful. You could be the best sleight-of-hand artist in the business, but if you do not use misdirection you will fail as a magician. Misdirection is a vital element of any magic trick.

Simply stated, misdirection is the psychological technique used to lead or manipulate the spectators' and volunteers' eyes and minds to see and believe what the magician wants them to. Their attention is focused in one direction while the trick is worked elsewhere. Misdirection is not pointing and saying, "Look at that!" and then doing something sneaky in the opposite direction. That is a crude form of misdirection that does not work well, nor does it leave a good impression with the audience. The techniques used by good magicians are subtle and sophisticated. So much so that the people in the audience never know they have been manupilated. With the proper use of misdirection you can stand in front of an audience and perform pickpocketing stunts without fear of detection.

Let's look at some of the primary misdirection techniques you can use to help make your pickpocketing successful.

ATTITUDE

One of the most important aspects of misdirection is your attitude. To properly manipulate people, you must win their confidence and friendship. You do this by being friendly and cheerful. If you are likeable, the audience will be less scrutinizing and more forgiving of mistakes.

If you convey an attitude that you are better than they are and try to impress them with how smart or clever you are, they will resent it. This kind of attitude breeds contempt, and audiences become defensive, suspicious, and critical of your actions and movements. Avoid looking like a showoff and you will have an easier time manipulating them.

ACTING

You must be a good actor in order to deceive your audience. If you've lifted an article and are casually holding it as though your hand were empty, you must make the audience believe it is empty by the position of your hand. It can be very obvious to everyone that you are holding or hiding something if your hand is not in a natural positon. The fingers may be curled too much or the wrist be twisted slightly too far. These signs will give you away and you may not be aware of it. Look at yourself in the mirror and examine the position of your wrist and hands when you are not holding anything. Try to imitate this postion *exactly* when you are palming a stolen article. All your actions must be natural in order to deceive and thus misdirect the audience. For example, you would never pull something out of your left breast pocket with the left hand; it is unnatural. You always do it with the right hand. Analyze all of your movements and make them all natural.

When you drop a stolen object into your pocket it must also be done naturally and without suspiscion. You must have a reason for reaching into your pocket, perhaps to pull out pixie dust to sprinkle around or to remove a hanky or some other item. As you reach into your pocket, deposit the lifted item and continue. You may also position your body while performing another trick so that you can easily drop the item into a pocket that is out of view of the audience.

Your face must never betray your actions. Sometimes when trying to do something sneaky, we clinch our teeth, poke out the tip of our tongue, blink, or do things that signal that something is happening. When you practice, ask someone to look at your face. Your facial muscles must be calm and impossible to read.

FORCE

As I've mention earlier, a stronger force will overshadow that of a weaker one. This is the most important misdirection technique you will use in picking pockets.

If you grab a volunteer's upper arm tightly, this will distract him as you simultaneously and gently pick his pocket. Whether you grab an arm, slap him on the back, tie a rope around him, or whatever, the force he feels must override that of your lifting. You should use this technique in combination with one or more other misdirection methods for best results.

THE EYES

Wherever you look and appear to focus your attention, so will the audience. Always look in a direction away from the pocket being picked. It will take practice to perform pickpocketing or any sleight-of-hand motion without looking.

This misdirection technique is strong enough to be used alone for some magic tricks, but in pickpocket magic you need to combine it with other techniques to make it effective. In fact, you should combine several misdirection techniques whenever you perform a trick. Doing so will make the deception better.

TIME

A great deal of the success you have in confusing and amazing your audience will result from your use of time. The time you allow to elapse from the moment you lift an item from a pocket to the presentation of the article to full view is important. Generally, people tend to believe that the steal is performed just before the article is revealed.

The longer you can allow the better. Picking the volunteer's pocket should be done when you are performing a totally unrelated trick. The audience nor the volunteer will not pay particular attention to your pickpocketing motions if they are unaware that this is your intention. Their focus will be on the trick you are currently performing. Allowing some time to elapse after lifting an article will erase all memory of you reaching into the volunteer's pockets earlier.

Always allow a certain amount of time to elapse between the accomplishment of a secret sleight or movement and its ultimate result.

You can also lead the spectators astray by making them think an affect is produced at a specific time, by a specific movement, when actually it had already been accomplished.

MOTION

The eyes always follow movement, particularly when it first begins. Lifting your hand, turning your head, moving your lips, bouncing a ball, are a few examples. As movements commence, the audience's eyes are naturally attracted to them.

For instance, if several people are seated in front of an audience and one is talking and using natural body gestures as he speaks all eyes are focused on him not on the others. He is the one with the movement. If one of the others makes motions larger than the first speaker, perhaps he begins speaking or stands up, our eyes will be drawn away from the first speaker and focus on the second.

Any sudden or unexpected motion will also quickly draw attention. The motion, however, must be natural or innocent to avoid suspicion.

The eye will always follow the hand that moves. You move one hand as a decoy as the other inconspicuosly works the magic. Be careful, if you have too much visible motion in your sleight-of-hand operation it will act as a magnet and attract everyone's eyes.

SURPRISE

One of the strongest forms of misdirection is the element of surprise. The best time to do a sleight-of-hand maneuver is at the same moment the results of a magic trick are exposed to the audience. At this time, the entire audience's attention is focused on the trick. The thought that something sneaky is occurring at the same time is beyond comprehension. Surprise will always cover a simultaneous subterfuge.

When presenting the climax of a magic trick, it is an ideal time to pick a pocket or work any type of sleight-of-hand. You must be quick, as the distraction effect only lasts a few seconds, and the pickpocketing must be performed simultaneously.

HUMOR

Silly antics and sight gags draw attention just as the suprise produced by the finish of a magic trick. Humor also makes the audience less critical. The audience's perceptions are relaxed, and they are not as analytical. Laughter keeps them off guard.

CONVERSATION

This is an excellent method when working with a volunteer. On stage you can use it effectively to distract your volunteer, but it must be combined with other techniques to fool the entire audience. When you look directly at someone and talk, people will usually look back, and their eyes are drawn away from your hands, giving you an opportunity to work your sleight-of-hand.

This effect is enhanced if you ask your volunteer a direct question and look him in the face. If you ask a simple, friendly, and unchallenging question he will look back into your face and focus his attention on his response. Avoid challenging or critical questions as they will cause him to be defensive and suspicious.

Besides asking questions, you can also direct him to do or say things that require effort and thinking on his part. Here are some examples:

"Are these yours?"
"What color do you see?"
"Choose any one."
"Look and tell me what you see."
"Say it loud and clear so everyone can hear."
"Turn this way."
"Step over here."

A steady stream of patter will keep the subject's mind occupied and oblivious to steals. Work on a monologue that will overload the volunteer's mind with patter, questions, and directions when you make your steals.

DISTRACTIONS

A spectator in the audience screams, an uninvited guest walks on stage, an accident occurs—these are all examples of distractions that will briefly take the focus off you so that you can work your magic. There can be no stronger misdirection than a distraction caused by a carefully planned accident. You are performing a trick and something falls over or you drop an object. Accidents are unexpected events that look unplanned and are thus beyond suspicion.

To drop, kick, stumble, fall, spill, etc., actually combines motion and surprise to attract attention. Be careful about using too many accidents or mistakes in an act or you may wind up looking inept. A clown magician, however, may be able to get away with using a lot of careless distractions since his character is supposed to be clumsy and silly.

3

YOUR AUDIENCE AND VOLUNTEERS

CHOOSING VOLUNTEERS

If you are going to pick pockets you are going to need victims, also referred to as volunteers. The type of people you choose is important. Avoid the clown or loudmouth who will want to steal the show or who will try to make your task difficult in order to show off and look clever. Although these types of people may get laughs, they will cause you problems and could ruin your routine. Also, avoid those people who appear shy or timid. These people will be nervous and uncomfortable on stage, and this will show in their speech and actions, making you and the audience uncomfortble as well.

You should choose people who are friendly, outgoing, and not afraid of getting up in front of an audience. They will go along with your instructions, have fun, and provide comic responses without trying to steal the show. Never choose a volunteer who is intoxicated or who appears to be a heckler or a show off. These types of people are hard to control and will make your life miserable.

Because all people are different and because you can never really tell how someone is going to act on stage, none of your shows will be exactly alike. Your routine may be identical, but the volunteers' responses will be different each time. Some will appear completely at ease while others will be somewhat apprehensive or nervous. Some will joke with you while others will be very serious. Some people are naturally funny just in their mannerisms and speech. Some people who appear to be outgoing in the audience may tighten up once they get on stage and are facing a large group of people. Therefore every show will be unpredictable to a certain extent and somewhat different.

Before the show starts, look over the audience for likely volunteers. You may choose those who are wearing articles of clothing or jewelry you can easily lift and who appear to have personalities suitable for your act. It is best to choose someone who is known by everyone or at least by several other members of the audience. Look for people who are part of a group. Choosing a volunteer from a group of people will enhance the audience's reactions to your stunts. The fact that someone the group knows is on stage makes it more enjoyable for the group and they will respond more freely. Their reaction will spark increased laughter among the rest of the crowd thus increasing everyone's enjoyment. The response is even greater if the subject you choose is a leader or popular member of the group. His friends will love to kid him about it later.

Rather than just choosing subjects from the audience, you may also ask for volunteers. Don't ask them to come up on stage or you will wind up with an overloaded stage or have undesirable subjects. Have volunteers raise their hands or stand up. Then make your selection. One advantage of choosing people who volunteer themselves is that you avoid choosing someone who is shy or who just doesn't want to participate. If you do select a person from the audience who hesitates and does not want to come up, politely choose another. Don't force him to participate if he doesn't want to. Chances are he would not be a good subject anyway.

WORKING WITH VOLUNTEERS

To get the best results from pick pocket magic you need to mix it with other effects, gags, and comic patter. Never announce to the audience or the volunteers that you are going to pick their pockets. If they don't know what you plan to do, they will not be suspecting you to pick pockets and when you do, they will be more surprised and your audience's reaction will be much greater. When you have a volunteer on stage, have him assist you in a magic trick unrelated to pickpocketing. This will give you an excuse to make physical contact with your volunteer without drawing suspicion from the audience or the volunteer.

It is very important that you get into the habit of touching your volunteers in a friendly and casual manner. Gently take their arm to lead them to certain parts of the stage. Pat them on the back, shake their hands, rest your hand on their shoulder while in friendly conversation, touch their arm or shoulder when you want their attention or response. Physically direct them as they help you perform a magic trick. By doing this, the volunteer becomes accustomed to your friendly physical contact and will not notice when you make a steal.

While the volunteer is absorbed in helping you with a trick, you can pick his pockets and remove wallets, pens, hankerchiefs, eyeglass cases, watches, jewelry and articles of clothing without suspicion. Keep these articles concealed until you reach a point in your act where you reveal your pick pocketing activities.

SECRET AND FULL VIEW STEALS

Steals can be made secretly so that no one knows about them or you can let the audience see you make the steal. If you secretly steal items from your volunteer and then produce them later as part of another trick or routine, you will completely confound and amaze your audience. Because so much can be done with stolen items, most of your steals will be in secret.

Letting the audience see the steal can introduce a great deal of humor so long as the volunteer is unaware of what is happening. After lifting an item, show it to the audience out of sight of the volunteer. Some steals can be performed in plain sight of the audience without the volunteer realizing what is happening. This lets the audience in on the gag. They become accomplices with you in deceiving your subject. This will increase their response and enjoyment.

GETTING CAUGHT

One of the major concerns you may have as a novice pick-pocket is what will happen if you get caught. This could be an embarrassing situation. Handled correctly, however, you can avoid embarrassment and continue with the stunt successfully.

What do you do if you get caught in the act of picking the volunteer's pocket? If the audience is still unaware of the steal, you can whisper to the volunteer to play along with you. Usually the volunteer will gladly comply. You then finish your routine as planned. Even though the volunteer is aware of the steal, if he plays along, your act will be well received and enjoyed.

If, on the other hand, when a steal is made and the volunteer openly exposes your actions, the only way to save face is to turn the situation into a joke. Turn the confrontation around to your advantage and make a funny gag or trick out of it. You can say that you need the item for your next trick. Have a "saving" trick planned for such an occasion. In this trick you use the item. Make it vanish or whatever to draw attention away from your attempted pickpocketing. The audience will soon forget about the steal and enjoy the trick and rest of the show. If you were attempting to steal the volunteer's wallet, for example, you might hand it to him and ask him to open it so you can borrow a dollar bill. (Never remove anything from sombody else's wallet. To avoid problems let them do it.) Do a simple trick with the dollar. During the trick, you may even attempt to steal his wallet again and, if successful, this can be very entertaining.

Another idea when attempting to steal a wallet would be to jokingly claim that it is *your* wallet and not the volunteer's. Offer to prove that the wallet is yours by stating that you always carry a special dollar with you—a magic dollar. Ask the volunteer if he has a magic dollar. He will deny having one. Hand him the wallet and tell him to pull out a dollar and give it to you. This will be the magic dollar. You then proceed to do a trick with the magic dollar. If done smoothly, the audience will believe it was all part of the act.

After returning the wallet or whatever item you tried to steal, you can attempt to steal it again later or steal another object.

If you have a saving trick, gag, or joke that you can use in case you get caught, you will be able to continue with the show without hesitation or embarrassment. Also, knowing that you have an "out" in case of detection will help you feel more confident, at ease, and less likely to make a mistake.

4

STEALING OBJECTS FROM POCKETS

Anything that can be placed into a pocket can be lifted without the owner's knowledge. The most difficult pocket to steal from is the back pants pocket where most men keep their wallet. It is difficult to steal from this pocket because the object rests close against the owner's body. Also, men are naturally sensitive to touch here because they carry valuables in this pocket.

Objects in other pockets are usually much easier to steal. In this chapter, instructions are give for stealing specific objects. If your volunteer does not have one of these objects but you want to make the steal, let him borrow the object and place it in his pocket.

STEALING A HANDKERCHIEF FROM
OUTER BREAST POCKET

First Method

Position the volunteer facing the audience. Stand behind him, and with your right hand, offer him something to hold in his right hand. Noticing that he is not doing it correctly, hold

his right hand with your right and raise his hand as high as it will reach. During this time, your left hand is resting on his left shoulder (see illustration above).

The left hand should apply some pressure on his shoulder and should not lie there lightly. The moment you begin to raise his right hand you say, "I want your hand up here." As soon as his hand is raised, press on his right hand, and pull up the handkerchief with your left hand over his left shoulder. The pull on the handkerchief should be a decisive one—one swift action.

Put the handkerchief into your pants pocket. The owner neither saw nor felt a thing, but in this case, you have allowed the audience to see what you did. This will produce a loud roar of laughter. The volunteer will naturally believe that the audience laughed due to your helping him up with his hand.

The misdirection here is perfect. Since he is concerned with his right hand, his eyes will be turned toward this hand, and will follow its movement upward. Your left hand presses on his shoulder with a purpose. When you pull the handkerchief away the volunteer will still feel the pressure of your hand there, or rather imagine it to be there, although it has moved away. Your right hand is holding firmly at the critical moment to ensure that the volunteer's attention is maintained on this side to cover the action of your left hand.

Second Method

In this method, the volunteer again faces the audience. Have him hold a tray or some other object in both hands. You bring a chair and place it behind him. Press down on both his shoulders with both hands, asking him to sit down. This is a natural gesture. You may have used it dozens of times in your home, in your office; in fact, anywhere else when inviting someone to sit.

Your right hand is in the correct position (see illustration on the following page). The fingers should be more toward the front side of the volunteer than toward the rear. As he bends to sit, pull away the handkerchief. Because he is moving in the opposite direction to the pull, the task becomes almost automatic. The handkerchief is disposed of in one of your pockets. The volunteer is again ignorant of what has transpired, but the audience knows—and they laugh.

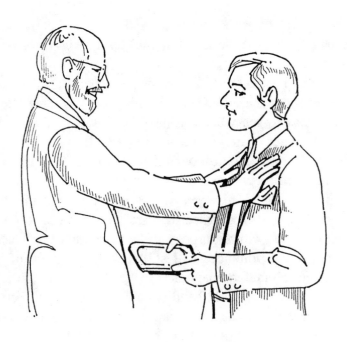

Third Method

In this method both the volunteer and the audience are in the dark. A table stands on the left side of the stage. The volunteer faces the audience. You stand beside him. Under the pretext of asking him to get something from the table or put something on the table, you hold him by his right forearm, your left hand again on his shoulder, and wheel him around so that his right side is now toward the audience (see illustration on the following page). Raise his right hand to about his shoulder height, then let go and point with your right forefinger toward the table. The moment you raise his hand, the right side of his coat is pulled forward by the action of his hand. This provides an additional cover to block the audience's view to the action of your left hand which pulls away the handkerchief. The moment the hanky is pulled away, your hand

travels to your side. Your body hides the hanky from the audience's view. The volunteer doesn't stand a chance of a look-in. The hanky is disposed of in your pants pocket.

All you have to remember in this kind of work is to execute the secret move under cover of some open action.

STEALING A PEN OR PENCIL FROM OUTER BREAST POCKET

This is the simplest thing to do. As a matter of fact, I used to do it out of devilment in my college days, when I could successfully get away with it. You can realize how easy an execution it must be.

The volunteer faces the audience. You are about to perform some trick. You find that he is too close to the front of the stage. Placing both your hands flat on his chest, you push him slightly backwards with the remark, "Would you mind standing back a bit?"

Your right hand goes right on top of the spot where the pen or pencil is; your left hand is at about the same level on the other side of his chest. What also is important, your head is turned toward your left for misdirection. As you press against him with both hands, get hold of the top of the pen in the crotch of your thumb, or, using a more technical term, in the "thumb palm position" (see illustration below).

As you move your hands away, grab the pen or pencil and it comes right out. The pull is slightly upwards and to the

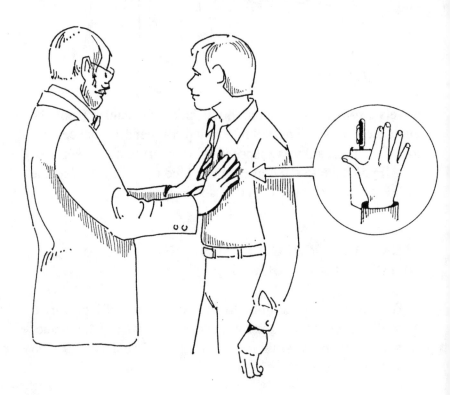

right. In a continuation of the same movement, your right hand goes behind him as you turn to face the audience, and the pen slipped into your pocket unobserved.

When you are turning to face the audience your right pocket will be away from the audience for a brief moment and this is the time to dispose of the pen. Here, the pressure of your hands against his chest will dull the sensation caused by the withdrawal of the pen. Let someone try it on you and be convinced.

STEALING A PEN OR PENCIL FROM INSIDE BREAST POCKET

Many people carry their pens in their inside breast pocket. Some unsuspecting reason must be found to get there before stealing the pen. So you work a vanishing trick, say with a card, coin or hank, it does not matter which. After the vanish, the article has to be recovered, so your left hand, with the concealed article, goes in search of it into his outer coat pocket and drops it in there. Pretending not to find it there, go inside the coat as if searching his inner breast pocket. The pen or pencil is lifted from the pocket, and under cover of the volunteer's coat, press it against your palm with the third finger.

Part of the pen, owing to its length, will naturally extend beyond the wrist. The hand is withdrawn in this position and the pen is kept hidden from view. The missing article not being found in the inner breast pocket either you now ask the volunteer to help in the search, and he eventually recovers it from his pocket. In the meantime, the pen is either dropped into your pocket or pushed through the front of your shirt. That is why I advocate using the left hand because by merely passing your hand in front of your shirt, the pen can easily be disposed of there. If you are wearing a vest, then the pen is pushed through the vest opening.

I will explain two other methods of disposing of the pen, but in these two instances the pen is disposed of before the hand is withdrawn from under the volunteer's coat. One method is to kick the pen up your shirt sleeve with the second or third finger after pulling it out of the pocket. The other method is to push it under your watch strap. If you are using the latter method, be sure that your strap or band is not too tight. It is, of course, understood that the last two methods are particularly recommendable when it is desired to have the hand free the moment it is withdrawn from under the coat.

STEALING MISCELLANEOUS ARTICLES
FROM INNER BREAST POCKET

People usually carry such things as wallets, driver's licenses, letters, etc., in their inner breast pocket. To remove the contents of this pocket, several trips will have to be made there. Vanishing a bunch of coins and pulling them out one at a time will serve the purpose, but I have found playing cards make the better medium.

Hand the volunteer a pack of cards for shuffling, but before doing so palm a portion of the pack. Reach into his pocket and deposit the cards, but bring out only one. This you hand to the volunteer to include in the pack for shuffling and you appear to be surprised how that card found its way into his pocket. To facilitate subsequent operations, the planted cards are loaded on the other side of the articles that may be lying in this pocket. The articles are allowed to remain near the body side of the volunteer. Two or three trips are later made to the pocket. Each time you search for a card, you palm an article out of his pocket. Every time you look for a card, you must bring one or more cards out, clearly visible between your

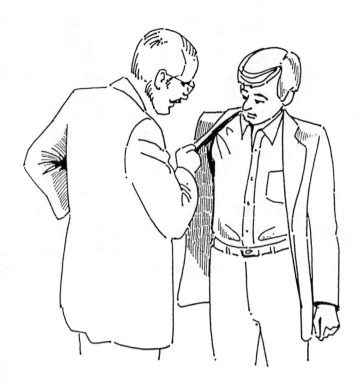

fingertips. The impression on the audience is that you are merely producing cards from his pocket.

Your position in relation to the volunteer is as follows: supposing you want to operate on his right inner breast pocket. He faces the audience and you are on his right side. When you reach into his pocket you will naturally have to turn your back partially to the audience. Your right hand goes in, palms an article and withdraws a few cards. As soon as the cards are withdrawn, you wheel slightly to the right in order to show the cards to the audience. This will take your left side away from the audience. After showing the cards, you pass them to the left hand, and incidentally, the hidden article goes with them. You turn again, this time not as fully as the first time and reach into the pocket again while your left hand drops the article into your pocket on the left side (see illustreation above).

In many instances you will find that it will not be necessary to palm out the articles at all. They are simply brought out behind the cards. Small articles like a driver's license, cigarette lighter, business card, and card case, etc., are all suitable. You can extract a wallet and other large articles if you get very close to the volunteer and pass it under cover of your body to the other hand. A word of caution is necessary here. On no account take out any loose change or bills. This will avoid a lot of complications later.

Once in each spot is enough, for the palmed article will have to be disposed of first before attempting it again, and this is best done when walking to another part of the theater. Since the audience they are witnessing only a feat of card production from the pocket, there is no reason for them to suspect otherwise.

STEALING FROM THE OUTER COAT POCKET

To steal from the two outer side coat pockets, it will not be necessary to go there openly as in the last case. Let us suppose you have designs on his right side pocket. You stand on his right, three-quarter of the way facing the audience. Your left side at this stage should be slightly behind the volunteer's body. You either work a body production here which you have previously loaded or go in search of something.

With your right hand, reach across his body and move the left side of his coat away, remarking, "Nothing there." Then take hold of the right side of his coat and move it towards you to expose the part of his body under the coat, and while pretending to look there expectantly, the coat front forms a wonderful screen for the left hand to operate. It is the simplest thing now for the left hand to take out anything found here (see illustration on the following page).

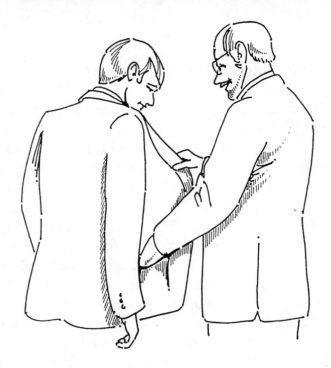

The disposal of the article is equally easy because of the position of your body. The lifted object is deposited in your left side pocket completely out of view. If operating on his left side, you naturally stand on the other side, and the right hand does the stealing.

It may appear to some readers that a lot of nerve is required to do this sort of thing. That is not so. If you were seated in the audience, would you suspect that anything other than what the magician appears to be doing is being done? No question of pickpocketing will enter the mind. A magician is supposed to put things secretly into a volunteer's pocket, not take them out. Besides, you are working under cover all the time.

The biggest secret to success is TIMING—TIMING—TIMING. This plays an important part in this kind of work, the same as it does in magic, swimming, running, or anything else for that matter. One may train his hands in sleights from now till Doomsday but if he does not have the sense of correct timing he opens himself up to detection.

STEALING FROM THE HIP POCKET

Here is an example I have used successfully in removing objects from the hip or back pocket. I have a little fun with this one and magically produce a pair of lady's nylon stockings from under the volunteer's coat. This gag never fails to produce a roar of laughter as well as hide my real intentions of stealing a wallet.

Before going on stage, hang a pair of lady's stockings under your coat at the back. Go on stage, and invite a volunteer to help you. You stand on the right side of the volunteer. Your left hand goes under your coat, grabs hold of the stocking, and moves under the coat of the volunteer. You are slightly behind the volunteer, so the movement of your left hand is well covered by your body as well as by that of the volunteer. Your right hand moves across the body of the volunteer from the front enters under his coat then moves around him to his left side, and takes the stocking. PRESS against the body of the volunteer with your right arm and body. In other words, you squeeze him in an embrace while your left hand relieves him of the contents of his hip pocket. This squeeze will dull the sensation that the movement of your left hand may have otherwise produced. The wallet is not withdrawn timidly or gingerly but JERKED out. After you gain possession of the wallet, your right hand slowly brings the stocking into view while the left passes the stolen goods behind the volunteer's back and sticks it under your belt unobserved.

Laughter is a wonderful complement to misdirection. In this example, the production of the nylons creates a humorous diversion for the volunteer and the audience. The hug or squeeze masks the volunteer's feeling so that his wallet can be removed without detection. I used the ploy of producing a lady's stocking, but you can, of course, use many different gimmicks or methods to accomplish the same goal.

5

STEALING A WRISTWATCH

This is one of those rare feats that creates real talk and publicity. Does it seem feasible? By all means, and it is no more difficult than the rest. There are four types of watch bands commonly which you may encounter—buckle bands, expanable metal bands, and two styles of metal clasp-type bands. After reading and practicing the following you will be able to remove a wristwatch without detection.

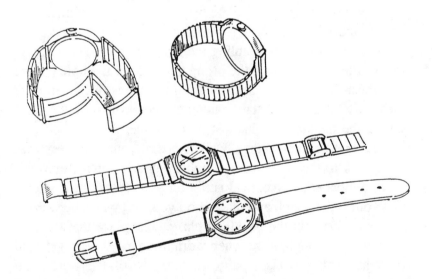

Common watch band types. Clockwise from upper left: metal clasp-type (one piece), expandable metal band, metal clasp-type (two piece), buckle band.

37

BUCKLE BANDS

This is the ordinary leather strap-and-buckle arrangement. One end of the strap is passed through the buckle and the prong in the buckle is passed through a hole in the end of the strap to keep it in position. This type of strap is similar to those used on leather belts (figure 1).

Buckle bands are the easiest for a pickpocket to work with. Using only one hand, you can grab the volunteer's wrist and candidly unbuckle and remove the watch.

To affect the steal, go into the audience and ask for someone to come up on stage. As the volunteer rises, get hold of his wrist with your right hand and hold him there with a strong grip. This is very important; your success depends 99 percent on this hold alone. Your hold position is as follows: the palm of your hand is directly on the face of the watch, the thumb and fingers on either side of the buckle (figure 2). This position comes second in importance.

While walking and leading the volunteer onto the stage, your thumb and fingers operate on the buckle. The fingers and thumb undo the buckle by first sliding the end of the strap out from the buckle, then doubling the strap over itself and applying a little pressure until the prong slips out of the hole (figure 3). Push the prong back away from the holes on the strap to prevent it from accidentaly catching when you slide the band out of the buckle. The hardest part is done.

As you get up on stage, walk ahead of your volunteer with your back to the audience and pull away the watch (figure 4). I can almost see a skeptical smile on your face, but it works. Get your wrist watch and place it on your left wrist, but for the moment, don't fix the buckle or clasp. Just place the watch in the position it ought to be when worn ordinarily. Now get hold of it as explained (i.e., palm on the face of the watch and fingers below), and press as hard as you can. Use your full

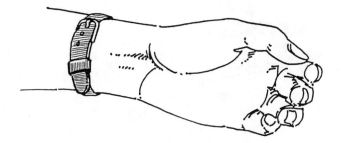

Figure 1

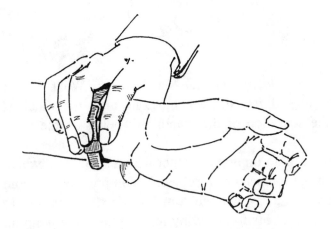

Figure 2

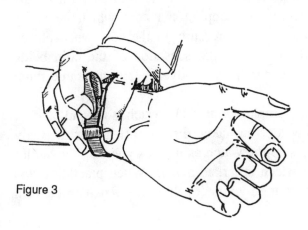

Figure 3

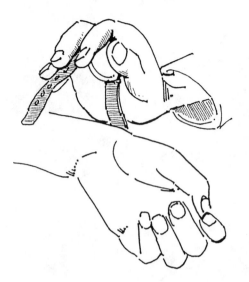

Figure 4

force, and then suddenly jerk the watch away. What do you feel? Do you still feel the watch? Long after the watch is removed, the sensation of the watch still being on the wrist persists.

Do you recall an impromptu stunt with a small coin which you stick on the forehead of a subject? You press on the coin and then draw it away without him knowing. He is told to drop the coin from his forehead by making his brow jump up and down. The coin is not there, but he continues for a long while in the attempt of dropping the coin which he really believes to be there. The pressure on the coin when placed against his forehead creates the sensation of the coin being present long after it has been removed. It is the same thing with the watch.

I would further emphasize that the watch is not pulled over the hand of the wearer but taken directly off his wrist. Only remember to press on the watch as hard as you can; the harder the better as the watch is jerked away. When practicing this steal, don't practice it on yourself. Strap the watch on the arm of a chair and, dragging the chair with you, count the paces taken before the watch is unfastened. With each repetition, try to reduce the paces until you come to the minimum. The chair should be a light one.

You can also remove the watch after you have come up on stage. To do this without leading the volunteer around on the stage, you will have him help you with a trick where you will grab his wrist with both hands. One hand will be positioned on the watch as described, the the other hand grabs the volunteer's forearm and serves as a distraction. Applying a greater force with the second hand will overshadow the feeling of the hand removing the watch. The watch is unbuckled and removed as described above.

EXPANDABLE METAL BAND

This is an elastic metal band which expands to fit over the hand. Although more difficult to remove than the buckle-type band, it can be done. With practice you can become very good at removing this type of band.

In order to remove an expandable metal band you will need to use both hands and cover your steal. Have the volunteer help you do a trick by holding an object in his hand. A small object like a coin, sponge ball, or scarf will make him clasp his hand into a fist and thus allow you to eventually slide the band over his clinched fist.

You remove the watch by first inserting a finger under the watch face (figure 5). With the fingers of the other hand, grab the opposite side of the band. Pull out with both hands to loosen the band from the volunteer's wrist. Spread the fingers so the entire band is no longer in contact with his wrist, and pull the band off over his hand (figure 6).

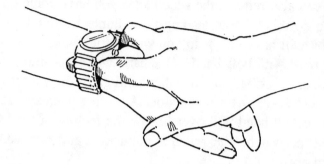

Figure 5

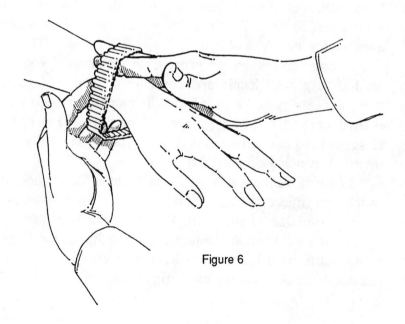

Figure 6

You can remove the band, but how are you going to keep the volunteer from feeling or seeing you remove it? You must preoccupy his mind with questions, directions and patter, and cover his hand so he cannot see what is happening. You can cover his hand with a tablecloth, scarf, boxing glove, etc., in the process of helping you perform a magic trick. You may also bind his hands behind his back (so he can't see what's happening) with rope or handcuffs. The application and removal of these objects can be used to mask the act of stealing the watch.

Work out a routine which will allow you to steal this type of watch. Stealing a watch is very impressive. Your audiences will love it.

CLASP-TYPE BANDS

Although not as common as the two types of bands discussed so far, another type of band which you may encounter is the clasp-type. There are two types of clasp-type bands. The clasp on one unloosens to make the band larger but is still intact. The other when unclasped divides the band into two separate segments (see examples on page 37).

Although the clasp itself is not too difficult to unfasten the first clasp-type band, because the watch does not expand or split into two separate staps, it is not easy to remove and is best left alone. You can, however, remove the second type. Once this clasp is loosened the watch easily slips off the arm.

You can remove this type of watch band using the same method as described for the buckle type bands. It is a little more difficult to unclasp this type of latch using only one hand but it can be done. You will need to experiment to find the hold and position which works best for your hand and fingers.

If you use both hands to undo the clasp this can be the easest band to remove. A simple lift of the clasp will accomplish your goal. You may have the volunteer do the same actions that allow you to remove expandable metal bands. The watch removal in this case will be easier since simply undoing the latch will surrender the band into your possesion.

6

STEALING ARTICLES OF CLOTHING

Stealing articles of clothing can make a hilarous climax to any magic act. Some articles of clothing and jewelry like suspenders, belts, cufflinks, tie clasps, necklaces, and bracelets can be removed without the victim's knowledge. Most articles of clothing, however, cannot be removed without detection. With a little trickery though, you can make it appear as if you can remove almost anything.

I will first explain how to remove a pair of suspenders from an unsuspecting volunteer. I will then describe how you can remove someone's shirt and most any other article.

STEALING SUSPENDERS

If anything could send an audience into convulsive laughter, this is it. Just imagine the effect on the audience when you pull a volunteer's suspenders right off as he is asked to return to his seat.

I will use coins for this example. In search of a missing coin, you reach under the volunteer's vest and under cover of looking for the coin, you undo the side buttons which hold the

suspender straps. Both your hands work together, one on each side, and the unbuttoning is done as swiftly as snapping the fingers twice. You don't interfere with the back buttons yet. Go into your routine, and when you are about to pull the suspenders off (after you have completed the trick he was helping you with), thank your assistant, and ask him to go back to his seat. As he walks away, reach under his coat from behind, both hands going there together, and with one move, the two back parts of the suspenders are unbuttoned. Pull down on the braces and it comes right clear from behind the coat in your hands. The volunteer will immediately get hold of his trousers fearing it would result in a calamity, and you, with the suspenders dangling in your hands, follow him.

This presentation can be very entertaining. You need a volunteer who is wearing suspenders. If you cannot find a suitable audience member to volunteer, you can still use the ideas presented here by using a confederate planted in the audience. Your assistant will wear suspenders and can liven up the act even more with exaggerated reactions and expressions. This same idea could effectively be used with an undershirt, boxer shorts or other piece of clothing. Of course, the clothing would need to be prepared beforehand so it could be easily taken off the "volunteer."

You can also work this as a gag with a real volunteer by concealing the article of clothing and pretending to magically remove it from your helper. Your volunteer will know that the article isn't his, but the audience will not, at least not at first. This type of thing can create a good deal of humor.

STEALING A SHIRT

A volunteer is chosen from the audience. He is wearing a coat, shirt, tie, and vest. Without warning, the shirt is suddenly jerked off from the startled volunteer. He is left with his tie, vest, and coat still in place but shirtless. The shirt and the volunteer are separated without harm although the volunteer may show signs of embarrassment. Like removing the suspenders discussed previously, the volunteer's response can be very comical.

To work this stunt you will need an assistant who is prepared beforehand and planted in the audience. The assistant will wear a coat, shirt, tie, and vest. The vest is optional, but if a vest is not worn the coat must be buttoned. Removing the shirt from beneath all these things makes the trick very impressive.

The secret to this trick is for your assistant to wear the shirt in a way that will allow you to jerk it from his body. The assistant, wearing only an undershirt on his upper body, places a dress shirt on top of his shoulders. The collar and first button of the shirt only come around the neck and are fastened. The sleeves of the shirt are laid across the top of the assistant's arms, and the cuffs are buttoned at the wrists (see the illustration on the following page). A tie is now placed around the neck and tied in the normal fashion. The front and sides of the shirt are laid in a fold over the shoulders and back. The shirttail is folded upward under the vest, which is then buttoned, and the coat put on. The shirt now appears to be completely normal.

The assistant enters the theater and sits with the audience. During the show you "randomly" choose him from the crowd to assist you with a trick. The assistant can come up on stage and sit in a chair or remain seated in the audience. Make sure to have him stand and face the audience as you talk to him so all can see that he is dressed normally. Explain to the audience that you will do the impossible, but don't tell them what you plan to do. The trick will have more impact if you keep them in suspense. Have your assistant loosen his tie and unbutton the first two buttons on his shirt and his cuffs. Loosen the collar and vest if necessary. Pull his shirt collar out from under his tie, and request for him to sit upright. With a firm grasp on the collar at the back of the neck, pull up. Draw the shirt up slowly at first, until you feel it release—then pull quickly. As the shirt comes free, hold it up for all to see. The assistant will respond with shock and embarrassment. As the audience is enjoying this surprise, give the shirt back and tell him to go get dressed.

STEALING ASSORTED OBJECTS

As a variation to this shirt stunt, you could remove the assistant's undershirt or shorts. Since these articles of clothing are not exposed to public view, their removal is very easy. The undershirt can be simply laid across the back of the shoulders out of sight underneath the coat. Undershorts can be tucked evenly into the back of the trousers. Make sure there are no unnatural lumps present.

Removing the shorts works best if the assistant is not wearing a coat, so the view is not obstructed. From behind your assistant, grab hold of the top of his shorts. Slowly tug and pull up on the shorts then, more quickly, jerk the rest of it out. This can be a very funny gag. You do the unexpected by grabbing the back of his shorts and end up with the whole thing in your hands.

The assistant's response is very important and can greatly add to the surprise and humor of this situation. You can have him exaggerate his actions and act like a clown (and an obvious plant), or he can be more mellow as if truly an audience member. A funny finish would be to hand him the garment and tell him to go someplace and put it back on. He grabs it and dashes out.

An assistant can be rigged up with various other articles of clothing or objects. Jewelry, watches, wallets, and other personal items can easily be made to look as if they were lifted off the volunteer by you. Some of these can be in your possession the entire time.

Here is one idea. You can hide items up your sleeve. Have the volunteer empty a pocket. After he is finished, state that he forgot something. Then reach in and pull out your hidden objects. You can have fun with this by pulling out such things as a fake rat, chicken egg, string of rubber sausages, etc. Be creative and use your own imagination and style to dream up ways to accomplish and present such tricks.

7

TRICKS OF THE TRADE

The secret to success in picking pockets is misdirection and applying a distracting force greater than that of your lift. A pickpocket on the streets must wait for the moment when his victim is preoccupied or his attention is diverted elsewhere before he makes his move. The magician, on the other hand, creates the misdirection and responds accordingly. The magician also has a legitimate reason for physical contact with the subject, unlike the criminal who must "accidentally" bump into or rub shoulders with his victim. And last but not least, the magician must time his actions appropriately. Misdirection, applying a distracting force, and the steal must all be in play at the same time in order to achieve success. The methods or techniques you use to accomplish this are not important, indeed there are countless ways to successfully work your pickpocketing. Use your imagination and devise your own form of presentation.

In the foregoing pages, I have explained how you can get into the different pockets of the volunteer. I have not mentioned anything about the front trousers pockets, as I prefer to leave that alone. The methods I have explained are not some theoretical possibility but the results of practical experience. When driving a car, each of us follows the same line of successive actions, but if the mannerisms of each are studied, it would show us that no two persons can be exactly alike. The hold on the steering wheel, the position of the legs and body in each case suggest individuality. While each driver is following the rules of driving, each applies them according to his own mannerisms and convenience.

I have set out the rules—the line of action—for you to follow. It is for you to apply this knowledge according to your own requirements. I have purposely not referred to the manner in which your hand should operate in the pocket, nor have I provided specific magic tricks to use in conjunction with the pickpocketing. I have not given you specific instructions on removing many items such as belts, cufflinks, bracelets, necklaces, etc. which can be removed without detection. But I have given you the basic principles of pickpocketing and ideas on misdirection and deception which will allow you to steal these items. As you practice in private, you will discover methods far more suitable to your mannerisms than any that I could show you. Anybody knows how to undo a button with one hand. It is far easier than fastening the button. Is it necessary for me to say to put this finger here and the other there?

Various techniques have been used to pick pockets. Street pickpockets have used many ingenious methods. One interesting method, although somewhat restrictive for the performer, is to use a false or third arm. The dummy arm is plainly visible and inconspicuous. While innocently standing near the volunteer, your real arm, which is concealed under your coat, can reach through an opening in the pocket and remove your volunteer's possessions. Since both of your arms are clearly in view and your attention is seemingly drawn elsewhere, the volunteer and the spectators are completely oblivious to your actions.

There are many ways you can design such an arm. You can even give the fake arm some mobility by using the concealed arm to manipulate it. The fake arm can be occupied by holding something such as a book or a hat, but clearly visible to all. You must also be able to put on and remove the third-arm jacket in a matter of seconds without anyone seeing you.

A less restrictive method and one that would be easier to perform would be to drape a cloth or some article of clothing over your arm. This is another technique borrowed from the street pickpocket. The material you use could be a tablecloth, cape, coat, etc., that you are using in one of your other tricks. Under cover of the cloth, you can extract the contents of your volunteer's pockets without fear of detection. Magicians frequently cover an object with a large cloth in order to perform a trick. Working this type of trick would give you an excuse for holding the cloth.

Be aware of opportunities that may present themselves. Many people go about with a handkerchief, paper or other things sticking halfway out of their pockets. It would be easy to pinch these. As you take hold of the article—you don't even need to pull it. He does it unconsciously for you, by walking away.

During your regular program, keep a watchful eye out and you will be surprised to see many undreamed of opportunities. While walking up the aisle in the audience for some reason or another, you have countless opportunities, especially with those seated on the aisle. I was extremely fortunate once in finding a lady's brooch on the floor of the theater. She had dropped it there when entering. You can imagine the publicity I got when later producing the brooch. The lady claiming it was seated right in the center of one of the rows of seats where I did not enter. By this I do not mean to suggest that if you look around you are going to find trinkets on the floor, but I do mean that you will see countless openings for your operation which had not entered into your earlier plans.

Pickpocketing can lead to good bit of comedy. You may have guessed while reading earlier sections that there are things you can do which will easily produce comic effects. Removing someone's suspenders is an example. You can also secretly plant objects in your volunteer's pockets or pretend to take them from him. Imagine the laughter you can get by slowly pulling out of the volunteer's pockets his underwear, a rubber ducky, a doll, or some other silly or unusual item.

In the next section I will explain how to "Deliver the Goods," that is, the manner in which items are returned to the owners. On this depends a great deal. Half of the fun would be lost if the articles were merely brought to light and returned. There should prevail the right element of SURPRISE which contributes in a large measure to the completion of the MYS-TERY.

8

DELIVERING THE GOODS

We now come to the most interesting part of the subject. It is here where the hounds are unleashed. Having completed your work with the assistant, or assistants, as the case may be, they are dismissed and asked to return to their seats. Suddenly it dawns upon you that you are going to do another trick and you ask for a handkerchief. Your remarks are directed to the fellow whose hanky you have pinched. He goes for his handkerchief and the expression on his face is enough to start the the audience to roar. If you have used a lifting method where the audience is in the know, so much the better, and the laughter increases. Say, "Never mind. I shall use one of mine." Here take out the hanky you have stolen. You appear quite innocent while handing it to him. The handkerchief has to be marked, so you call for a pen. This is missing also, and you pull his pen out of your pocket. It is immediately recognized. In the minds of the owners, it appears as if you have stolen these items just before calling for them and not much earlier, as the case might have been. Addressing the owner of a wallet, for instance, you ask for the loan of a bill. He goes to his pocket, but you immediately take the wallet out and ask, "Is this what you are looking for?"

In the case of a cigarette case, offer a cigarette to the owner. The moment he sees the case, he goes to his pocket to ascertain whether his case is there or not. You remark, "Well, never mind. You may have mine." The cigarette lighter is shown casually to the owner with the remark, "I wonder what this cost?" In the case of the suspenders, hold up and say "What am I bid for these?" These are just a few ideas. Each article is brought to light with some excuse.

Now the magician with the greater imagination always takes full advantage of any situation. He makes his work appear far stronger than it really is, so here we employ a ruse. In your pocket, you already have a few articles of your own. Suitable articles are such things as a man's undershorts, a sock, a lady's garter, in fact, such articles that cannot be removed easily under even the most favorable conditions. Don't have too many of them. Two or three are more than enough, and for most of the time only one such will suffice.

Here is a part which always works great just before pulling the suspenders off your volunteer. Before removing the suspenders, hand the lady's garter to this man and tell him it belongs to that lady over there. "Will you please hand it to her?" Point at some imaginary spot. As he moves away, you pull the suspenders out. He forgets the garter and his hands go straight to his waist to hold up his trousers. The imaginary spot to which you point must be one of the spots which you have been to earlier in the program otherwise, nobody will believe it. To make it more realistic, in passing that way earlier accidentally drop something near a lady and pick it up. When the garter is brought out later, the "clever" ones will at once recall this incident and figure that the accident was specially arranged and the garter was really stolen then. Besides, who would expect a lady to lift up her skirt in public in order to disprove you? You are, in any case, not pointing to any particular individual.

With the sock, for instance, just walk down into the audience and address a man saying, "Don't leave without this." Whatever the reply, you hand the sock to him. The audience will draw different conclusions, and since this raises more laughter, that is all that matters.

With the underwear, I proceed as follows: When you pull off a pair of suspenders, naturally everyone starts laughing. So you bring out the underwear and hand it to someone whom you see laughing quite loudly and remark, "One can't be too careful, you know." If he does not accept it, naturally the laughter increases. All this helps the situation and many such ruses will suggest themselves to the operator.

Articles belonging to one person can later be discovered in another's pocket. The handkerchief which the audience saw you pinch earlier is secretly loaded to another person's pocket or under their coat, and here the audience, while sharing your earlier secret, is equally mystified when it is later produced from elsewhere. With the greatest of ease—and I mean greatest of ease—articles stolen can be dropped into the pockets of people sitting on the aisle. Get near a person under some pretext—you have to be close to him—and the hand that is closest to him does the work. Another way is to ask him to stand up for some thing or another, or during a card trick, to hold up a card to show to the audience. Your hand naturally touches him gently on the arm which he is resting on the arm of the chair. You drop the small article to his pocket and gently help him up. Your body makes a natural cover to assist this operation.

In all such transfers from one pocket to another, one has to remember to allow some time to elapse before the final recovery or discovery. The detective attributes his success to the power of linking one isolated incident with another. We magicians, in order to evade detection, always destroy the means of connection. Spectators assume the secret of the trick was worked just prior to its presentation and mentally may try to discover the magician's secret by retracing his most recent actions. The spectator, however, will not be able to find the connection and usually dreams up some wild rationalization to solve the mystery. Most magic tricks are very simple, much more so than people realize, however, because of the presentation, they appear almost supernatural and quite sensational! Picking pockets is wonderful in this respect. Handled right, as I've described, you can deliver both a humorous and astonishing demonstration.

9

TRAINING TECHNIQUES

You are going to have to become familiar with picking pockets before actually attempting it. For most other types of magic, you can just stand before a mirror and repeat the same move over and over again. You do not need any outside help. But for picking pockets, you will need an assistant to rehearse the operation. It is not so easy to find a good helper. The person on whom you may be practicing may soon get fed up. He has no interest in the work. I tried it with several boys to act as dummies, even paying them by the hour, yet they got fed up standing there "for no reason at all," as some have said to me. So what do you do?

You can go through the necessary practice in the privacy of your own bedroom using a dummy volunteer. This is what I did. If you can get hold of one of those tailor's dummies, so much the better, but that is not absolutely necessary. Get a table and place it before your mirror. Now find a chair and place that on the table with the seat side facing front. The highest point of the chair should coincide with about shoulder height of the average person and this can be adjusted by getting the right size of table. Hang a coat on the back of the chair the same way as you naturally do. Now this outfit represents your volunteer, and you can go at it for all you are worth.

Just to convince you of the effectiveness of this procedure, I can modestly claim that this outfit has helped me to learn how to put in and remove objects from under the coat of a volunteer to such a degree of perfection that I am able to work it as close as a couple of feet away from the audience without being caught.

As you practice, work into it the other tricks, patter, and misdirection techniques you will use. In order to be a successful pickpocket, you will need to practice the diversionary techniques that will allow you to empty someone's pockets without being noticed. Practice with the dummy until your movements are smooth and natural and your routine convincing. Naturally your routine and patter will continue to evolve with time and practice.

Once you have practiced with your dummy volunteer and have the moves and routine down to perfection, you will need to test yourself on a real live person. It is easy to fool a dummy, but it will take a bit more practice to deceive a living, feeling person.

Try it on a friend at first. Don't tell him you're going to pick his pockets. Use misdirection and patter just as you would on stage. You can tell him you need his help to practice some unrelated magic trick you've been practicing and then, under the guise of that trick, pick his pockets clean.

If you succeed in deceiving your friend, you're on your way to becoming a successful pickpocket. If your friend catches you picking his pockets, simply explain to him what you are doing and ask him to help you practice. Have him help you improve your technique and practice on him asking for his feedback. If you can pick his pockets without him feeling or seeing you, even when he is conscious of what you are trying to do, then you will be successful. Always practice your steals on a friend before performing them in public. He can provide you with helpful comments to improve your technique and give you actual practice with a living human being.

You will need to practice each steal you make. Concentrate on only one at first. Work on it until you have it mastered and can perform it well. Then learn another steal and master it and so on. In time you will be able to perform several pickpocketing stunts and can combine them for added effect.

Picking pockets can create some startling effects and riotous laughter. The first public applause and appreciation you receive when performing pickpocket magic will give you a great deal of satisfaction. After your first public presentation you will understand more about its worth than I could tell you in fifty years.

For a catalog of other unique and fun books write to:
PICCADILLY BOOKS
P.O. Box 25203
Colorado Springs, CO 80936 U.S.A.